# Iona Abbey
## and Nunnery

*Anna Ritchie and Ian Fisher*

*'That man is little to be envied, whose patriotism would not gain force
upon the plain of Marathon, or whose piety would not grow warmer among the ruins of Iona.'*
(Dr Samuel Johnson, October 1773)

*Approaching Iona across the Sound from Mull.*

Iona, of all the many sacred places in Scotland, is an enduring symbol of Christianity. St Columba arrived in the island with twelve companions in AD 563 and founded a monastery that was to become the heart of the Scottish Church during its early years. One of the most important monasteries in early medieval Europe, it was a renowned centre of learning and artistic excellence with extensive international contacts. Despite repeated attacks by the Vikings, the monastery and the sanctity of the island survived. The gravestones of early monks can still be seen, along with the magnificent high crosses that show the skills and learning within their monastery. The foundations of the little stone oratory known as St Columba's Shrine may mark the original resting place of the saint himself.

The peaceful graveyard of Reilig Odhráin was the burial place of both monks and warlords in early times. St Oran's Chapel was added in the twelfth century, probably to house the grave of the great Somerled, 'king of the Isles'.

Around 1200, Iona became the scene of massive building operations. Somerled's son, Reginald, led a move to transform the Church in the West Highlands and bring it into line with developments throughout Europe. A Benedictine abbey replaced the old Columban monastery, and an Augustinian nunnery was built at a discreet distance. Close to the nunnery, the little chapel of St Ronan's (Teampull Rònain) was rebuilt as the parish church at around the same time. The tracks between all these places of worship were well trodden in medieval times by locals and pilgrims alike, and a wayside prayer-cross, MacLean's Cross, was set up in the later decades of the fifteenth century at a point where the tracks meet.

Around the same time, another bout of major building works got underway, with the aim of improving the abbey church and extending the domestic buildings of the nunnery. But this new era of prosperity was not to last for very long.

The Scottish Reformation of 1560 put an end to monastic life in Iona and the abbey and nunnery gradually fell into the picturesque ruins so popular with the tourists of the eighteenth and nineteenth centuries. The nunnery remains a ruin, but the abbey was restored to new life during the twentieth century.

As a modern tourist you are continuing the long tradition of pilgrims travelling to Iona from afar.

*From the ferry, the visitor walks up through the village.*

# A Guided Tour

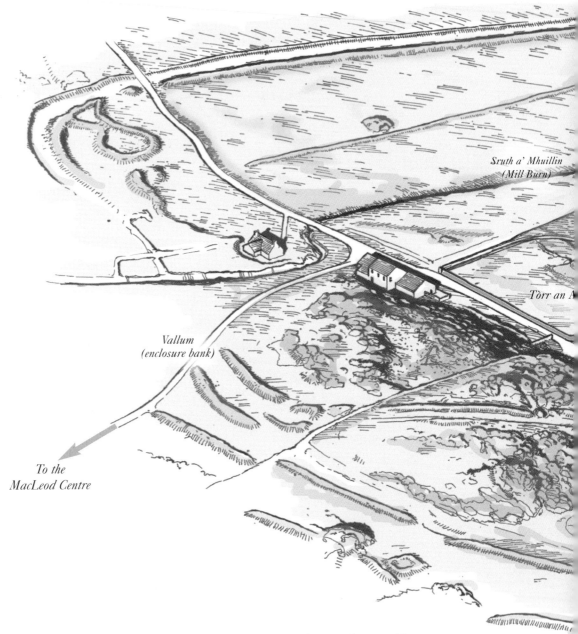

*Sruth a' Mhuillin (Mill Burn)*

*Tòrr an A*

*Vallum (enclosure bank)*

*To the MacLeod Centre*

This guidebook takes the reader on a guided tour of Iona Abbey and Nunnery, highlighting the most significant features of interest. Thereafter the extraordinary story of St Columba and his wonderful legacy on Iona is revealed.

The visitor sees the abbey restored and alive. That this is so is a tribute to the many people who in recent times have not only revered its ancient sanctity but also believed it had a vital role to play in our modern world, as a place for calm and quiet reflection.

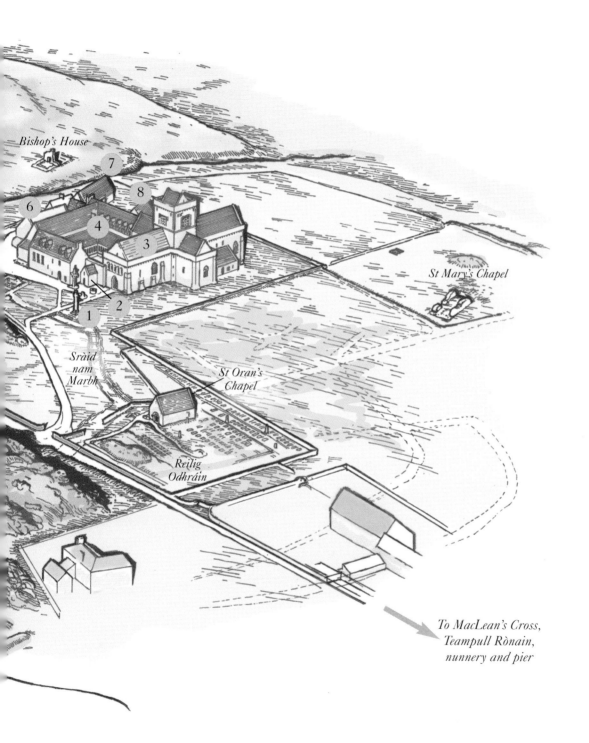

| 1 | The High Crosses | 5 | Bakehouse |
| 2 | St Columba's Shrine | 6 | Abbot's House |
| 3 | Abbey Church | 7 | Abbey Museum |
| 4 | Cloister | 8 | Michael Chapel |

Bishop's House

7

6

4

8

3

St Mary's Chapel

2

1

Sràid
nam
Marbh

St Oran's
Chapel

Reilig
Odhráin

*To MacLean's Cross,
Teampull Rònain,
nunnery and pier*

*On top of Tòrr an Aba is the stone socket for a medieval cross.*

*The rocky knoll of Tòrr an Aba rises in front of the abbey.*

# Tòrr an Aba,
# St Columba's Legacy

Start your tour on or beside the little rocky knoll, known traditionally as Tòrr an Aba (Gaelic for 'hill of the abbot'.) This is a good place on which to stand and absorb the remains of the abbey complex.

Here Columba is believed to have had his writing-hut, from which he could see out over the Sound of Iona to Mull. From this spot it is possible to follow the line of the vallum (or enclosure bank and ditch) that, from the seventh century, swept in a great protective arc around the Columban monastery. It ran west from the sea near St Mary's Chapel, between the graveyard Reilig Odhráin and the abbey, thence north around the low hills behind you and back east to the sea at the far side of the field to the north of the abbey.

Although most of the vallum is now lost to sight, we know that the main buildings of the Columban community lay within its boundary. They included at least one church, the saint's shrine (the small chapel immediately ahead of you, now between the church and the cloister), accommodation for monks, guests and pilgrims and many of the domestic, agricultural and industrial buildings which served the community. There is scant evidence of the layout of these buildings but there seems little doubt that the Lord of the Isles chose to place the medieval monastery in a position that showed respect for the earlier sacred buildings. It is likely, therefore, that the Columban church lies under the present church.

*The cobbled Sràid nam Marbh ('street of the dead') leads towards the abbey.*

# Sràid nam Marbh

Below Torr an Aba you will see a cobbled track threading its way through the grass from Reilig Odhráin, the graveyard, towards the abbey church. This is the only section of Sràid nam Marbh, 'the street of the dead', to survive; the track along which the coffins of kings and chiefs were carried in ancient times formerly reached back to Port nam Mairtear, 'the port of the dead', beyond the present pier.

# The High Crosses

Between Sràid nam Marbh and the abbey church you will see two high crosses (one now a replica) and the stump of a third. A fourth once stood in Reilig Odhráin. All four crosses date from the eighth and ninth centuries, and are probably the last survivors of a much larger number of crosses, some perhaps made of timber, that marked the pilgrims' route from the landing-place to St Columba's Shrine. They would also have served as places to pause and pray.

St Martin's Cross, furthest from the church, is the sole intact survivor. It was sculpted from a single stone slab imported from the Argyll mainland. The west face (facing away from the church) is carved with scenes from the Bible, whilst the side facing the church is richly adorned with bosses and serpents. The slots in the ends of the short side-arms once held wooden or metal decorative mounts.

The solid granite stub closer to the church is St Matthew's Cross. It was probably erected a century or more after St Martin's Cross. More of the cross is on display in the abbey museum.

The impressive cross standing closest to St Columba's Shrine is a replica of St John's Cross. The original is also in the abbey museum. With a span of almost 2.2 m, it is one of the widest crosses known in the British Isles. Originally it was a ringless cross, and thus structurally weak. The four segments of ring were probably added early on in an attempt to strengthen it. Nevertheless it would seem that it collapsed soon after its erection.

Even its recent history makes sorry reading. In 1927 the fragments were stuck together with cement and re-erected. But this too was blown down in 1951, and again in 1957. It was then decided to take the fragments to the abbey museum. The present concrete replica was set up in the original stone base in 1970.

*St Martin's Cross was sculpted from a single slab of stone imported from the Argyll mainland sometime between 750 and 800. This east face is richly carved with bosses and serpents.*

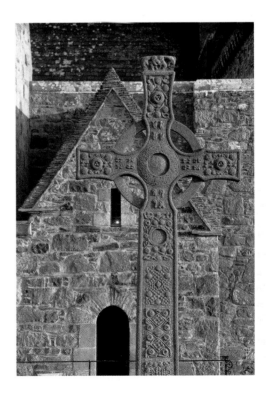

*The replica of St John's Cross in front of St Columba's Shrine.*

# St Columba's Shrine

The little stone building to the left of the west door into the church is known as St Columba's Shrine. Most of the walls were restored in 1962, but the lowest courses are original and may date back to the ninth century. The building was an oratory or chapel built to an Irish design (where the long side walls project). The tradition linking it with Columba may well preserve ancient knowledge of where the saint had first been buried.

Originally the building was freestanding, and it was left that way even after the medieval abbey was built, so respecting its antiquity and sanctity. Indeed, the medieval church may have been built in its present position to demonstrate a relationship to the shrine. The ancient track, Sràid nam Marbh, used to pass through the gap between the shrine and the church, until that gap was finally closed in the fifteenth century when the angle-tower was added to the church.

*Daniel flanked by lions.*

*Abraham with sword raised to sacrifice Isaac.*

*Virgin and child.*

*David plays the harp beside a musician playing the triple pipes.*

*David with Goliath and David with Saul.*

*Twelve serpents writhe around six bosses.*

*Faint traces of an inscription - it may have recorded the name of the abbot or wealthy patron who commissioned the cross.*

*The west face of St Martin's Cross is carved with scenes from the Bible.*

*The shadow of St John's Cross falls across St Columba's Shrine.*

9

# The Abbey

*The abbey church from the south today.*

*The abbey at the end of the nineteenth century, just prior to restoration.*

# The Church

Enter the abbey church through the west door. You are now in the world of the medieval Benedictine monks.

The church was the most important building in the abbey; it was where the monks spent much of their day in prayer or attending one of the eight daily services. It also had to accommodate the many ceremonies and processions usual in a monastic community, as well as the demands of pilgrims and the local congregation. The architecture of the church had, therefore, to reflect these functions.

As you can see from the plans, the church underwent several transitions between its construction around 1200 and its abandonment in the seventeenth century. The original plan took the form of a cross. A square **chancel** at the head of the cross housed the high altar, the arms of the cross, known as transepts, and the central crossing provided space for the monks' **choir** and additional altars, while the shaft of the cross formed the **nave**. But scarcely had this work been completed than changes were being carried out to the east end. The changes surely reflect the growing throng of pilgrims visiting St Columba's resting-place.

Firstly, between 1220 and 1250, the chancel was moved further east and the choir extended well to the east of the crossing tower. Narrow side aisles were added to north and south. Then, later in the century, the short south transept was replaced by a much grander one, though it was probably never completed. About the middle of the fifteenth century, it was the turn of the nave to be altered when the south wall was rebuilt further south and a new west front constructed. Around the same time, the south transept was reduced to something like its original size and a new south aisle added to the choir.

The church remained like this until the abbey became derelict after the Reformation of 1560. An attempt in the 1630s to restore the eastern part to serve as the Cathedral of the Isles was short-lived, and restoration to its present state was not achieved until the twentieth century.

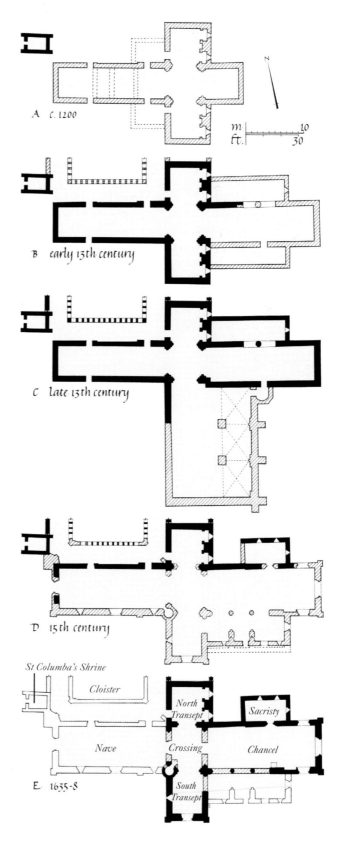

*How the shape of the church changed between the thirteenth and seventeenth centuries.*

# The Nave

*Distinctive crosses were carved onto the walls when the church was consecrated.*

Always the most public part of the church, the nave is a simple rectangular space without aisles. Two processional doorways lead north out to the cloister.

The nave was the only part of the medieval church that needed extensive rebuilding in 1909-10 (see the photograph on page 44). The upper parts of the south and west walls, including the distinctive five-light west window, belong to this period. The lower parts, including the west doorway and small north-west angle-tower, are part of the major fifteenth-century rebuilding. A small window in the angle-tower overlooks the nave doorway.

Inside the west doorway, the squared sandstone masonry of the west wall of the narrower early-thirteenth century nave is still visible. An irregular scar south of the porch marks where the original south wall was until the fifteenth century. Part of the wall lies under a grille beside the font.

The unusual change in floor-level appears to be a fifteenth-century innovation. The north wall had been almost entirely demolished before the modern rebuilding, but the lowest stones in both doorways remain. Traces of three walls have been found below the floor of the nave; these may represent part of the early Christian church.

*The font in the nave, gifted in 1913, is made from Iona marble.*

# The Transepts

The north transept is the only substantial part of the original Benedictine church of AD 1200 to survive. It is late Romanesque with Irish and Scandinavian influences, such as the small wide-splayed windows and plain round-headed arches with moulded bases and capitals, one of which preserves its foliage ornament. Against the west wall rises the reconstructed night stair, down which the monks filed direct from their dormitory for the night-time services. Queen Elizabeth gifted the oak screen in the crossing-arch in 1956.

*The nave, looking east, towards the crossing and choir.*

*The north transept looking east. Between the two chapels, each lit by a single window, is a niche for a statue. This may have been a representation of St Columba, but only the feet now survive.*

# The Crossing

The crossing dates mainly from the fifteenth century, but the high north arch of the earlier crossing remains visible above it. The massive two-storey tower is reached by a steep spiral stair in the south-west corner. The upper storey housing the belfry and a pigeon-loft is not normally accessible for safety reasons. It is lit by elaborate traceried windows that can best be viewed from outside the church. The clock on the belfry window replaces an earlier medieval clock, and the large bell was cast at Loughborough, England, in 1931.

An inscription on the south pier of the east crossing-arch names the principal carver of this fifteenth-century work, who was perhaps also the master-mason: DONALDUS O BROLCHAN FECIT HOC OPUS ('Donald Ò Brolchán made this work'). Is he perhaps the face looking down on you from the west crossing-arch?

It is worth pausing to examine the fine carving on the south crossing-arches and continued on the capitals of the arcade separating the choir from the south choir aisle. They show biblical scenes, mythical animals and foliage as well as depictions of contemporary life, including an armed rider and foot-soldier, and an intriguing cow-killing scene.

*The intriguing cow-killing scene, carved on one of the capitals at the crossing.*

*Does this capital perhaps record the name of the master-mason?*

13

# The Choir

*A carved capital in the choir.*

Because of its importance in the working of the church, the choir is that area that has seen most change down the centuries. Amid the rather confusing array of features the sequence of developments can still be made out.

The extent of the original chancel is indicated by the moulded sandstone string course that extends along the north wall for about 5 m from the crossing to the dogtooth-enriched double arch. (You will see it above the present choir stalls.) The base supporting the central circular column of the double arch marks the floor level of the extended and raised choir of c.1220-50, almost 2 m above the present floor. The two arches once gave access to a north aisle. Beneath the choir itself was an undercroft, or basement, with a timber ceiling supported on a stone ledge, parts of which are visible below the west arch and below the north choir window. Quite how this raised choir worked is not clear. We do not know how many steps were required to access it, or whether they ran across the full width of the choir.

The reorganisation carried out in the fifteenth century saw the removal of the raised choir and a return to the original floor level. The double arch was blocked up and the present elaborate doorway inserted partly within the east arch to give access to a sacristy beyond, where the altar vessels, vestments and furnishings were stored. The work also included the east end of the choir, the entire south wall, the south choir aisle and south transept, as well as the tower over the crossing.

The new chancel at the east end was lit by three large windows of flamboyant style reminiscent of Irish work. This area was the presbytery, reserved for the clergy officiating at the celebration of the mass. Near the south window are a piscina (a basin where the altar vessels were ritually rinsed), and a triple-seated sedilia (where the priests sat) carved with foliage ornament in West Highland style. The modern communion table is of Iona marble; the original marble altar was destroyed by souvenir-hunters in the eighteenth century. To either side are stone effigies clothed in their ecclesiastical vestments, the one attributed to Abbot Dominic (1421-c.1465), who initiated the fifteenth-century rebuilding, and the other Abbot John MacKinnon (1467-c.1498), the clan chief's son.

*Clergy sat in these seats during services.*

*The sacristy doorway has a beautifully carved arch.*

15

*The sunlit cloister was a quiet place for the monks to linger in contemplation.*

# The Cloister

In monastic houses throughout western Europe the buildings in which the monks lived and worked were grouped around a central court or cloister. The four covered alleys linked the church with the domestic rooms, but they also served as a place for quiet contemplation and as part of the processional route around the abbey.

The lean-to roof of the cloister is supported on an arcade formed of pairs of octagonal columns with moulded bases and capitals decorated mainly with scalloped and water-leaf ornament. Numerous original fragments are preserved, but only a few were in good enough condition to reuse during the restoration of 1958-9. Many of the new column capitals are carved with bird and foliage designs.

Most of the buildings around the cloister are substantial modern rebuildings of ruined medieval fragments, or in the case of the west range entirely modern. They are also actively used by the Iona Community and for that reason are largely inaccessible to visitors. Specific highlights to look out for include, off the east cloister alley, the **chapter house**, where the brethren met daily to read a chapter from the *Rule* of St Benedict, discuss business and confess sins; the original stone bench seats around the walls survive. In the north-east corner is the **day-stair** that led up to the monks' dormitory on the upper floor of the east range, and in the north-west corner is the former **refectory stair**, now blocked but once quite an elaborate feature. The **undercroft** below the refectory now serves as the abbey gift shop.

*A modern sculptor, Chris Hall, at work in the cloister.*

## The West Highland Graveslabs

Around the walls of the cloister is one of the abbey's special highlights, the magnificent collection of West Highland graveslabs. They demonstrate a local style of stonecarving developed at Iona in the fourteenth century and known as 'the Iona school'.

The effigies were made to commemorate 'the best men of all the Isles', the leading members of the West Highland families, including MacDonalds, MacKinnons, MacLeans and MacLeods. They bear distinctive foliage-ornament and often swords, hunting-scenes and other figural panels. Most were removed from Reilig Odhráin and placed here for their better protection and safekeeping.

## Beyond the Cloister

Facing you as you emerge from the west side of the cloister is a low ruin, now paved, planted with flowers and furnished with seats. This was the site of the monastic **bakehouse** and brewhouse. The cobbled Sràid nam Marbh runs up to its south doorway. Turning to your right and skirting round the modern west range, you will pass the **abbot's house** (heavily restored) and glimpse the ruined **bishop's house**, on the far side of Sruth a' Mhuillin, 'the mill burn'. Thought to have been built in the 1630s when the abbey church enjoyed a brief new life as the Cathedral of the Isles, the bishop's house was described by early visitors as having a large living hall 'open to the roof' with a kitchen beyond and bedchamber above.

*One wall of the
Bishop's House
stands proud.*

*Bread and ale were made in the bakehouse (the ruined
building in the foreground now a garden), well away
from the cloister to avoid danger of fire.*

# The Abbey Museum

The restored building beyond the abbot's house may once have been the monks' infirmary, or hospital. It now serves as the **abbey museum** where much of the abbey's wonderful collection of carved stonework is now housed. (Work is currently underway on conserving and redisplaying the collection, and as a result there may be occasions when the museum is closed.)

A particular highlight of the museum is the reconstructed St John's Cross that formerly stood close to St Columba's Shrine, together with the surviving fragments from Iona's two other ancient high crosses, St Matthew's Cross and St Oran's Cross.

St Oran's Cross is thought to be the earliest, closely followed by those of St John and St Martin; all three date within the middle or later decades of the eighth century. St Matthew's Cross was constructed about 100 years later. Their decoration is similar to contemporary metalwork and manuscripts, notably the *Book of Kells* (see page 35), which may have been made by the monks of Iona. The high crosses are part of a highly developed and accomplished artistic tradition that draws inspiration from Ireland, Pictland and England.

St Oran's Cross originally stood in Reilig Odhráin. It was made in three pieces: shaft, side-arms and top-arm, each fitting its neighbour with a mortice-and-tenon joint. It is decorated with serpents and bosses, the Virgin and Child flanked by angels, and a figure with a lion who may be David, Daniel or Jerome.

*St John's Cross as it is preserved in the museum.*

*This drawing shows how St Oran's Cross once appeared.*

# The Michael Chapel

South of the abbey museum is the **Michael Chapel**, a small chapel that was part of the early thirteenth-century abbey. It may have served as the monks' temporary place of worship whilst building work progressed on their abbey church. The windows date from around 1500, and the whole chapel was fully restored in 1959, thanks largely to donations from Africa; the stalls and curved ceiling are of African timber.

# St Mary's Chapel

As you walk around the east end of the abbey church, you will see the ruins of **St Mary's Chapel** in a field beyond. This too probably dates from around 1200, and may have been used by pilgrims as they waited for the abbey church to be completed; a medieval track ran past the chapel.

# The Vallum

When you reach the road again, and before you visit Reilig Odhráin and St Oran's Chapel, make a detour along the road to your right. After passing the Iona Community's Coffee Shop and crossing the mill burn, on your left you will see the best-preserved stretch of the **vallum**, the earthwork that once enclosed the early monastery and later the abbey - an area of around 8 hectares. It consists of a deep ditch between two substantial banks. Even in its weathered state, the drop from the top of the inner bank to the bottom of the ditch is fully 4 m - such was the dividing line between the secular world and the spiritual one inhabited by Columba and his successors.

*Inside the Michael Chapel.*

# Reilig Odhráin

St Oran's Cross and many early Christian gravestones, most now in the abbey museum, have been found in Reilig Odhráin, which suggests that it was in use earlier than the twelfth-century chapel. Fine medieval effigies and graveslabs once marked the burials of the leading families of the Isles. Kings from Scotland and Ireland were also buried here, although it is not certain how many or exactly where. King Lulach, MacBeth's stepson, was the last to be laid to rest on Iona, in 1058. By the time Lulach's successor, King Malcolm III, died in 1093, Iona was to all intents and purposes Norwegian territory, and Malcolm and his successors were laid to rest in a new royal mausoleum at Dunfermline Abbey, Fife, in the very heart of the kingdom of Scotland.

*The gravestone of John Smith (d. 1994), the former leader of the Labour Party, lies in the north-east extension of Reilig Odhráin, added around 1990.*

*St Oran's Chapel surrounded by ancient burials in Reilig Odhráin.*

# St Oran's Chapel

St Oran's Chapel, restored in 1957, was probably built as a family burial chapel either by Somerled, 'king' of the Isles, who died in 1164, or by his son Reginald.

Somerled and his successors ruled over a vast area, from the Isle of Skye in the north to the Isle of Man in the south. Somerled himself was killed at Renfrew by the Scots, after having led an invasion fleet gathered from his sprawling 'empire' up the Clyde estuary. His grandson, Donald, founded the mighty MacDonald clan.

Irish influence can be seen in both the architecture and the decorative doorway of this fine building. Inside is an elegant tomb-recess, built in the late fifteenth century, perhaps by John, the last Lord of the Isles.

*The twelfth-century doorway into St Oran's Chapel has fine chevron ornament.*

*A monument in Reilig Odhráin raised to sailors drowned in the treacherous waters around Iona.*

*The late-medieval tomb-recess inside St Oran's Chapel was probably built to house the body and effigy of John, the last Lord of the Isles, who died in 1503.*

23

# MacLean's Cross

This fine cross was erected around 1500 beside the ancient Sràid nam Marbh, 'street of the dead', at a point where it met another track leading up from Port Ronain, 'St Ronan's port', where the modern pier is today. We can picture pilgrims filing up from the boats and pausing to say a prayer here before moving upwards to the abbey itself.

The cross is a fine example of the Iona school of stonecarving of the late fifteenth century (whose output included also those wonderful graveslabs now on display in the abbey cloister and museum). Carved from a single stone slab more than 3 m high, it stands in its original socket-slab on a modern base. The armed horseman carved on the foot of the shaft may be a depiction of the MacLean chief who commissioned the monument.

*MacLean's Cross is decorated with tightly packed plaitwork and foliage. Two animals are featured just below the cross-head on this east face.*

*The west face has a very weathered carving of the Crucifixion scene.*

*MacLean's Cross with the present parish church and manse beyond. Teampull Rònain served as the parish church in medieval times.*

# Teampull Rònain

Teampull Rònain, 'St Ronan's Chapel', was the parish church of Iona from around 1200 until the sixteenth century, when the Reformation left the island with no place of worship until the present kirk (beyond the field beside MacLean's Cross) was built in 1828. Restored in 1923 and again in 1993, it is a very plain building, and perhaps surprisingly small for the population of the island. However, medieval churches did not have seating, and the chapel could hold quite a few people standing.

Excavation beneath the floor in 1992 revealed traces of an earlier, and even smaller, chapel, perhaps dating to the eighth century. Beneath were burials of even earlier date. These show that there was a lay population on the island contemporary with Columba's monastery.

*Excavation in progress beneath the floor of Teampull Rònain in 1992.*

# The Nunnery

The great building enterprises of around 1200 included this nunnery. Earl Reginald, its founder, installed his own sister, Bethoc (Beatrice), as the first prioress. Although ruined, the nunnery is one of the best preserved in Britain. Such houses were common in Ireland, and it is likely that many of Iona's first nuns were Irish.

Like their male brethren in the abbey, the nuns followed a life of contemplation and prayer. They lived off the income from the modest land holdings they were granted by their patrons, on Iona and adjacent islands. Although we know little about them as individuals, it seems they were not held in high regard in the fifteenth century, probably because they were often caught in the crossfire of land disputes. Nonetheless, lay women of noble birth were brought to the nunnery for burial from far and wide, a tradition that continued until long after the nunnery ceased to function at the Reformation of 1560. An elaborate double-ended graveslab (see page 40), a memorial to Prioress Anna MacLean, who died in 1543, was badly damaged when the roof of the chancel collapsed in 1830.

The **church** consists of a nave with an aisle of three bays on the north side, a small chapel at the east end of the aisle, and a chancel, originally separated from the nave by a wooden screen. The north chapel has a fine triangular-headed window of Irish type and a rib-vaulted ceiling. The chancel also had a rib-vaulted ceiling. The church was embellished with carving, some of which can still be seen on the capitals of the nave-arcade and on the corbels that supported a timber gallery inserted at the west end of the nave around 1500.

The **cloister garden** is a scented and tranquil place to linger on a summer's day. Clues in the surviving masonry suggest that the nunnery was enlarged in the fifteenth century, although the original cloister may have been smaller than the 14 m square that exists today. It is sad to think that only a few decades later the Reformation put an end to its activities. Only foundations of the cloister arcade now remain, but surviving fragments in the abbey museum show that it was beautifully decorated.

The **east range** contained three rooms at ground level, including the chapter house with stone benches around the walls. The nuns' dormitory was on the upper floor.

The **south range** consisted of a large refectory where the nuns took their frugal meals. In the sixteenth century, the east part of the refectory was adapted for domestic use by the insertion of an upper floor.

The **west range**, which now lies largely under the modern road, probably provided guest accommodation.

*Chap...*

*Teampull Rònain*

*The nunnery ruins from the north-east with the ferry pier beyond.*

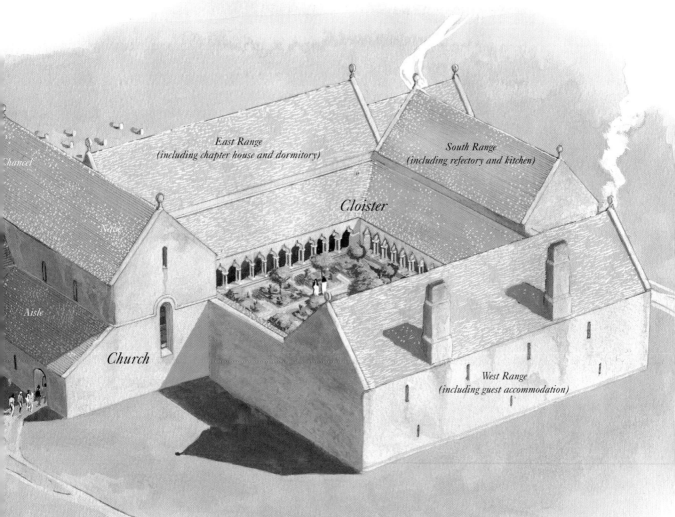

Chancel

East Range
*(including chapter house and dormitory)*

South Range
*(including refectory and kitchen)*

Cloister

Nave

Aisle

Church

West Range
*(including guest accommodation)*

*The arrangement of the nunnery accommodation (David Simon).*

# The Story of Iona

*'I saw his island of Iona. Though I have never been there in the flesh,
yet in the Spirit I could see it, bathed in the bright light of angels.'*

(Adomnán of Iona, *Life of St Columba*)

*The island of Iona seen from the south. The abbey and nunnery are towards the top right, and the sandy bay in the right foreground is Port a' Churaich ('port of the curragh, or coracle'), or Columba's Bay, where the saint is traditionally believed to have landed. (Courtesy of Colin Baxter Photography.)*

# Before Columba

The name Iona is thought to derive from 'eo', the old Irish word for a yew tree, and it is possible, but not yet proved, that yew may have been prevalent here in Iron-Age times 2000 and more years ago. Pollen analysis has shown that, at the time of the early Columban monastery, oak, ash, birch, willow and probably hazel were growing on the island but that the oak and ash were swiftly decimated by tree clearance, both for their timber and to improve the farmland.

Iona is a small island and its economic resources were always limited, but a reasonable living could be made on land, supplemented by the rich harvest from the sea. There is fertile land along the north-east of the island, where Columba founded his monastery, and across the middle of the island, known as 'the green belt', to the sandy grasslands fringing Camus Cùl an t-Saimh, 'the bay at the back of the ocean'. In these areas cereal crops could be grown and cattle pastured. The plentiful seaweed made a good fertiliser for the fields and could even be burnt as a fuel.

Although Iona is close to Mull, the islands are quite different in bedrock and topography.

Sandbanks and fast tidal currents make the Sound of Iona treacherous to navigate. In the past, all this made Iona more isolated than it looks on the map, yet also more dependent on Mull and the adjacent Scottish mainland for supplies, especially timber and good stone for building and carving.

There is just one Iron-Age fort on Iona, on Dùn Bhuirg, 'the hill of the fort', at the north end of Camus Cùl an t-Saimh. Dùn I, 'the hill of Iona', the highest on the island, has no trace of fortification on it. This suggests that the people of the island belonged to one tribe with a single warlord as their chief, with his residence on Dùn Bhuirg. The fort had a stone wall along the landward side of the hill (the steep seaward side needed no defence) and small round stone houses. Excavations have produced pottery and glass beads dating from the first century BC to the third century AD, but the hill may have been occupied for longer. Even if it had been abandoned before the sixth century, it is most unlikely that Columba found Iona empty of residents when he arrived in AD 563.

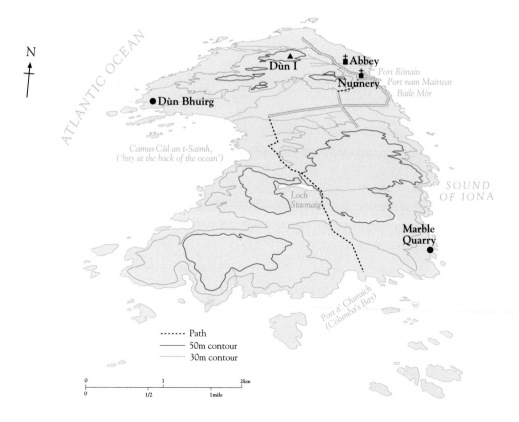

*'The Coming of St Columba', by William McTaggart (1835-1910). (Courtesy of the Trustees of the National Galleries of Scotland.)*

# Columba - Saint and Statesman

The man called Columcille (Irish for 'Dove of the Church'), but better known to us by his Latin name Columba, was born of royal lineage in County Donegal, Ireland, and trained in the newly-introduced monastic life from an early age. He founded monasteries in Ireland before leaving for Iona in AD 563. His departure from Ireland attracted many legends, including one story that he had illegally copied a Bible-manuscript and started a war against the king who had ordered its return, and that he vowed never to see Ireland again.

When Columba arrived in 563, Argyll, or Dalriada as it was known, was ruled by a Gaelic-speaking aristocracy of Irish origin, known as the Dál Riata, after whom it was named. Columba stayed initially with the high king of the Dál Riata, Conall mac Comgall, before taking up residence on Iona.

Columba and his companions landed, according to tradition, at Port a' Churaich, 'the port of the curragh, or coracle', at the south end of the island. The curragh was a light but immensely seaworthy vessel with a wooden framework over which animal hides were stretched and sewn. The vessel was then greased to make it watertight. If you visit Columba's Bay today, you will see, in the pebble shingle well back from the sea, about 50 cairns of many different sizes. These are thought to be the work of pilgrims over the centuries, commemorating both Columba's arrival as well as their own.

Columba and his monks travelled widely throughout Dalriada, founding churches both on the mainland and the islands. His royal descent gave him the authority to deal as an equal with kings in Dalriada and Ireland, and with the rulers of neighbouring peoples, including those of Strathclyde and Pictland. In 574, he ordained Áedán mac Gabhráin as king of Dalriada at Iona, in one of the first Christian inaugurations in western Europe.

Yet this great traveller and statesman was also a dedicated church leader, portrayed by Adomnán, his biographer, as a model for the pure monastic life. Columba spent most of his last 34 years on Iona, copying manuscripts, meditating, and leading his monks in worship and daily work. He was accessible for practical and spiritual advice to lay visitors as well as to his community, and imposed penances on offenders. The highlight of Adomnán's *Life of Columba* is an account of the saint's last weeks, when he blessed each part of his beloved island, its crops, livestock and people, before his death in the half-lit church, at midnight on 9 June 597.

*An artist's impression of the burial of St Columba, and (above) St Columba's 'pillow' now in the Abbey Museum. The stone 'pillow' was once thought to have been where the holy man laid his head each night (David Simon).*

# Iona
## Icon of Christianity

*This graveslab, on display in the Abbey Museum, was designed to lie flat above a burial. Note the similarity in design with the* Book of Kells *(opposite).*

Columba's monastery on Iona was founded by a small group of men for whom the early years must have been an endless round of hard physical work, building, digging and clearing the land. Archaeological excavations around the abbey have uncovered traces of the earlier monastery, and Adomnán's *Life of Columba* mentions some of the buildings both of his own and Columba's time.

The monastery was enclosed by an earthwork, or vallum, within which were the church with a side-chapel, a guesthouse, a communal building where the monks probably cooked and ate their meals, and their sleeping quarters. It is not clear whether this was a dormitory or separate huts, but Columba certainly had his own sleeping-hut. He also had a writing-place, likely to have been on Torr an Aba, 'hill of the abbot'. References to fetching timber from Mull and gathering reeds suggest that the buildings were chiefly of timber and thatch, and archaeologists have found the remains of wooden buildings, including traces of open-air workshops for metalworking and glass making, together with debris from leather working and woodworking.

Columba's monastery continued to flourish long after the saint's death in 597, and its fame was such that in the eighth century at least two Irish kings retired to spend their last days there. By then the monastery would have had a scriptorium, in which the monks copied sacred books and illustrated them in glowing colours and with wonderful designs. The magnificent gospel-book, the *Book of Kells*, is thought to have been created on Iona before being taken to Kells, in Ireland, for safety in the early ninth century. The monks also kept an annal, a list of notable events occurring over the years. The original manuscript does not survive, but part of it covering the period from the early seventh century to about 740 was incorporated into the *Annals of Ulster*.

*The bank of the monastic vallum, or early enclosure, still rises high in places.*

*Christ enthroned - one of the richly-coloured paintings in the* Book of Kells.
*This superbly-crafted gospel-book may well have been created in Iona's scriptorium.*
*(Courtesy of the Board of Trinity College Dublin.)*

*Viking warships dominated the western seaways in the ninth and tenth centuries.*
*(Courtesy of the Pierpoint Morgan Library, New York, MS M. 736, f. 9v.)*

# Vikings

Just 200 years after Columba's death on Iona, the western seaways held a new and unexpected menace - the longships of Viking raiders from Norway. Monasteries were targeted for their treasures of gold and silver church plate, and Iona suffered particularly savage Viking attacks in 795, 802, 806 and 826, and periodically thereafter into the late tenth century.

Iona somehow managed to survive these onslaughts, mainly by a strategy of partial withdrawal. In 804, the abbot and monks acquired land at Kells, in County Meath in Ireland, and built a new monastery there, to which they could betake themselves and their treasures as necessary. These included the famous *Book of Kells*. From now on, the abbots of Iona were as likely to be in residence in Kells as Iona, if not more so.

Around 840, the Viking menace brought about the union of Columba's Scots with their erstwhile enemies, the Picts, to the east, and certain relics of Columba found their way there also. These included his crosier, removed to the safety of Dunkeld, then the principal church of the new united kingdom (St Andrews took precedence only from the eleventh century).

*Dunkeld Cathedral, Perthshire, where St Columba's relics were taken in 849.*

Perhaps the most famous Columban talisman to survive is the *Brecbennach*, a casket made in the eighth century and said to have contained relics of the holy man. Around 1200, it was given into the safekeeping of the abbot of Arbroath and in 1314 was carried into battle against the English by Robert the Bruce at Bannockburn. The casket is better known today as the Monymusk Reliquary.

*The Monymusk Reliquary, made in the eighth century, is believed to have held relics of St Columba. (Courtesy of the National Museums of Scotland.)*

Yet somehow, despite all the violence, a monastic community of sorts continued on Iona. The Vikings were even ultimately imbued with the spirit of Columba and became Christian themselves. In the abbey museum are several gravestones of the late tenth and early eleventh centuries recording the deaths of Christian Vikings - one runic inscription translates as: 'Kali the son of Olvir laid this stone over his brother Fugl'.

# Somerled and the Lords of the Isles

There may well have been a small community of monks on Iona when Somerled, 'king of the Isles', held sway in the early twelfth century. Somerled's very name, meaning 'summer warrior', betrays the fusion of Norse and Gaelic blood that was the legacy of the Viking era in the Scottish Hebrides. From his powerbase in Argyll, Somerled won a naval victory in 1156 over the Norse king of Man to gain control of the southern Hebrides. His descendants, the MacDougalls of Lorn and the MacDonalds of Islay, dominated the region for centuries thereafter, ruling from such mighty castles as Dunstaffnage, near Oban.

Yet these great warlords and seafarers were unrivalled among the barons of Scotland as monastic patrons. Somerled himself, in the very year of his death (1164), invited a reforming Irish abbot to Iona, and either he or his son, Reginald, founded Saddell Abbey in Kintyre for Cistercian monks. About 1200 Reginald brought both Benedictine monks and Augustinian nuns to Iona, and about 1230 his nephew, Duncan MacDougall, founded Ardchattan Priory on Loch Etive.

The 'sons of Somerled' inevitably became embroiled in the diplomatic and military disputes between the kings of Scotland and Norway over the sovereignty of the Hebrides. They played a cunning game, until the battle of Largs in 1263 effectively ended Norway's overlordship.

In the wars of independence from England that raged after 1296, MacDougall power declined because they threw in their lot with the English against Robert the Bruce. But the authority of the MacDonalds grew as a result of Angus MacDonald's loyalty to the Bruce. Angus's son, John, reunited the southern and northern Hebrides by marriage, and from 1354 he used the title 'Lord of the Isles' in memory of his ancestor, Somerled.

*The great bulk of Dunstaffnage Castle, north of Oban, ancestral seat of the MacDougalls of Lorn.*

The Lords of the Isles governed with the advice of a council, which included the abbot of Iona and the bishop of the Isles based on Lismore Island, off Oban. Many of the great chiefs, among them MacKinnons, MacLeans and MacLeods, were brought to Iona for burial in Reilig Odhráin, and their impressive crosses and monuments can still be admired today.

St Oran's Chapel, probably built for Somerled himself, continued to serve as the burial place of the Lords of the Isles until the late fifteenth century. They remained generous benefactors to the abbey throughout; Earl Donald, for example, who died in 1421, had a precious shrine made for a part of St Columba's hand. But in the 1490s the Lordship, weakened by family feuds and years of wrangling with the Stewart kings of Scotland, was finally declared forfeit by James IV. The title, Lord of the Isles, was thereafter bestowed on the heir to the Scottish throne, the Duke of Rothesay, and future attempts by the MacDonalds to regain their lost title and lordship proved futile.

*Effigies erected on Iona of warriors underline the importance of the leading families of Argyll and the Western Isles.*

*The presence of oared galleys, or birlinns, on many of the Iona gravestones reflects the importance of the sea and inland lochs in the lives of the West Highland chiefs.*

# Benedictine Monks and Augustinian Nuns

Reginald, Lord of the Isles, invited Benedictines monks and Augustinian nuns to Iona about 1200. Benedictine monasticism took its name from St Benedict of Nursia, who drew up rules for the guidance of his monks at the monastery of Monte Cassino, in southern Italy, around 525, a generation before Columba arrived on Iona. Benedict's rules were designed for a life of poverty, chastity and obedience, and were gradually adopted for other monasteries.

The first Benedictine community in Scotland is thought to have been that established at Dunfermline, Fife, soon after 1070; Iona was the last of five more such monasteries founded in the country. The Benedictines were also known as the 'Black Monks' because they wore black habits.

The Augustinian order followed the teaching of St Augustine of Hippo, in Egypt, who died in 430. They were less rigidly organised than monks, and the canons (though not the nuns) could act as priests for the local lay population. The first community in Scotland was established at Scone, the ancient Pictish king-making centre in Perthshire, around 1120. A number of others followed, including at Scotland's main cathedral, St Andrews. Iona, though, was one of only two houses of Augustinian nuns established, the other being at Perth. The Augustinian nuns too wore black habits, and their nunnery church on Iona was locally called *an eaglais dhubh*, 'the black church'. The abbey church was simply known as *an eaglais mhor*, 'the great church'.

*Only part of Prioress Anna MacLean's gravestone (died 1543) survives today, but this drawing of 1772 shows the complete stone with the Virgin and Child.*

*John MacKinnon was abbot of Iona from 1467 to about 1498. His effigy, in the abbey church is carried on the backs of lions.*

# The Daily Round

Although other functions such as practical charity, hospitality and education came to be associated with monastic foundations, their prime purpose was seen as creating beacons of prayer in a sinful world. To this end there was a perpetual round of services, starting at about 01.30 and continuing until the monks and nuns retired to their dormitories around 20.00. Their day and night revolved around eight set services, or offices, known as *Opus Dei*, or 'The Work of God', comprising psalms, anthems, prayers and readings.

These offices were interspersed with celebrations of the mass and other services particular to the time of year or to the importance of a certain day in the calendar. After the first mass of the day, the community met in a room adjacent to their church, called the chapter house, where a chapter from their rule was read (hence its name) and where they confessed their sins and conducted business.

Between services there was time for spiritual, intellectual or even manual activity. The gardens had to be tended, books written, meals cooked, guests looked after, and patients in the infirmary cared for.

# Pilgrims' Progress

*'..a consecrated place, resplendent with Divine favour'*
Jerry O'Sullivan

It is difficult to overstate the importance of pilgrimage to Iona. We should not see it simply in the context of the single focus at the shrine or church, but as a circuit of the many satellite pilgrim stations, outlying chapels, burial grounds (at least nine existed on Iona), hermitages and holy sites associated with St Columba's many miracles, culminating at the shrine of the saint.

Early pilgrims may have travelled to the island in the same kind of curragh as Columba. They would have landed at Port nam Mairtear ('port of the martyrs') or Columba's Bay. All came in a heightened emotional and spiritual state. Their progression around the circuit would have culminated at St John's Cross and the tiny Shrine immediately behind to pray for themselves and their families. They came because, as well as possessing

miraculous powers, Columba's relics became known as symbols of spirituality. The relics were not exclusively fragments of his human remains but included his tunic, hand-bell, pastoral staff and gospel-book. Even when the Viking raids necessitated the removal of the relics for safe keeping, Iona still attracted pilgrims. The Benedictines encouraged pilgrims, although the only relic recorded on the island was the 'hand of St Columba'.

The original focus of medieval pilgrims was probably in the north transept, for the central niche on the east wall presumably contained a statue of the saint, perhaps accompanied by a reliquary shrine. This area may have been set aside for the reception of pilgrims until the east end of the church was remodelled in the thirteenth century. The upper level of the extension would have provided sufficient space for a shrine chapel behind the high altar.

*An artist's impression of pilgrims wending their way towards the shrine of St Andrew at St Andrews Cathedral, in Fife (David Simon).*

This remodelling also included large aisles on the north and south of the choir, allowing a one-way route for the pilgrims, possibly with a two-storey arrangement of shrine altars, via stairs formed in the aisles. This form of architecture can also be seen at Whithorn and Glasgow, where similar cults were encouraged. It provided a heightened dramatic setting for the cult along with a number of opportunities for veneration.

An attempt to extend the reception area for pilgrims to the south in the later thirteenth century was over-ambitious and failed. However, in the early fifteenth century, Abbot Dominic set about rebuilding the church, prompted by the collapsing timberwork of the choir. In 1428, he petitioned the Pope to grant an indulgence of three years off purgatory to all pilgrims visiting Iona on Columba's feast day, thereby boosting the abbey's income to help pay for the construction work. Pilgrims were a major source of income for the abbey and the nunnery, which no doubt provided guest accommodation for highborn ladies travelling as pilgrims.

After Charles I's failed attempt to re-use the east end of the church as the Cathedral of the Isles in the 1630s, the buildings fell into ruin. The island was without a church for the first time in a thousand years.

Martin Martin, Scottish explorer and author, came to Iona late in the seventeenth century and described the abbey as 'anciently a seminary of learning, famous for the severe discipline and sanctity of Columbus'. Clutching a copy of Martin's book, Johnson and Boswell followed a century later. Johnson said 'We were now treading that illustrious Island, which was once the luminary of the Caledonian regions, whence savage clans and roving barbarians derived the benefits of knowledge and the blessings of religion'.

*The shrine of St Patrick's hand. A similar Columban relic existed on Iona. (Courtesy of the Trustees of the Museums & Galleries of Northern Ireland.)*

43

# The Abbey Restored

In 1874-6, the eighth Duke of Argyll, who owned the entire island, commissioned the celebrated architect, Robert Rowand Anderson, to consolidate the abbey ruins. Then in 1899, the Duke transferred ownership of the abbey, Reilig Odhráin and the nunnery to the newly established Iona Cathedral Trust, committed to restoring the church for public worship. Despite misgivings on the part of several architectural historians, and despite the fact that the Trustees had to raise every penny of the funds needed for the work, the restoration was underway in 1902 and the first service was held on 14 July 1905 in the partially restored church. Work on the nave was completed in 1910.

A new era in the rebirth of the abbey began in 1938 with the establishment of the Iona Community by the Reverend George F MacLeod, minister of Govan Old Parish Church in Glasgow. This was an innovative scheme to bring together craftsmen and trainee ministers to work on

*The abbey as it is today.*

*The abbey at the end of the nineteenth century, just prior to restoration work beginning.*

rebuilding the abbey, with the longer term aim of preparing young ministers for the rigours of working in deprived inner city areas. Restoration of the monastic buildings began immediately, using designs by Ian G Lindsay, and was completed in 1965 with the building of the entirely new west range to the cloister.

The island of Iona was bought from the trustees of the Argyll Estate in 1979 by the Fraser Foundation and given to the nation in the care of The National Trust for Scotland. MacLean's Cross had long been in state care, and in 2000 the Iona Cathedral Trust relinquished care of the abbey, Reilig Odhráin, Teampull Rònain and the nunnery to Historic Scotland.

*Reverend George F MacLeod. (Courtesy of the Iona Community.)*

*Marble effigies in the abbey church commemorate the eighth Duke of Argyll (who died in 1900 and is buried at Kilmun) and his third wife, Ina McNeill, buried here in 1925.*

# A living Community

Today the restored abbey church and cloister are in daily and lively use. The Iona Community takes responsibility for the leading of morning and evening worship, and in the summer months a short early-afternoon service for day visitors. The north transept includes displays reflecting the Justice and Peace commitment of the Iona Community. In addition, visitors will often hear a pianist or singing group practising, or see the sacristan preparing the church for the worship of God, which is after all the reason this wonderful building exists.

As tenants of Historic Scotland the Iona Community, and staff working here on its behalf, welcome guests each week. Forty-five people (as well as staff) can stay in the abbey cloister, and a similar number at the MacLeod Centre nearby. There is also an outdoor adventure centre at Camas on Mull. These are not retreat centres, or hotels, but places where guests are invited to share for a whole week in work and worship, and to discuss issues of the day, or learn about the environment of the Hebrides or the history of Iona. One day each week is spent on a pilgrimage round the island.

The Iona Community is an ecumenical movement, with a radical theology. There are about 250 members, from all the major Christian traditions in Britain, lay and ordained men and women, with a wide range of ages and occupations, dispersed throughout the British Isles and beyond.

The Community also has a mainland base, in Glasgow, where the leader is based and from where the Community's programme of youth development work is coordinated. The Wild Goose Resource Group, also based there, is well known for its music and work on renewing congregational life through worship, with the aim of 'finding new ways to touch the hearts of all'. Many songs now well known in Scotland were first sung here in Iona Abbey.

*Invisible we see you, Christ beneath us.*

*With earthly eyes we see beneath us stones and dust and dross, fit subjects for the analyst's table.*

*But with the eye of faith, we know you uphold.*

*In you all things consist and hang together: the very atom is light energy, the grass is vibrant, the rocks pulsate.*

*All is in flux; turn but a stone and an angel moves.*

*George F MacLeod*

*Modern-day pilgrims to Iona gather round St Martin's Cross.*

## FURTHER READING

Ewan Campbell *Saints and Sea-kings: the first kingdom of the Scots* (1999)

Thomas Owen Clancy and Gilbert Márkus *Iona: the earliest poetry of a Celtic monastery* (1995)

Ian Fisher 'Early Christian archaeology in Argyll', in Graham Ritchie *The Archaeology of Argyll* (1997)

Ian Fisher *Early Medieval Sculpture in the West Highlands and Islands* (2001)

E Mairi MacArthur *Columba's Island: Iona from past to present* (1995)

Anna Ritchie *Iona* (1997)

Royal Commission on the Ancient and Historical Monuments of Scotland *Argyll: an Inventory of the Monuments, vol 4*, Iona (1992)

Richard Sharpe *Adomnán of Iona: Life of St Columba* (1995)

Peter Yeoman *Pilgrimage in Medieval Scotland* (1999)